DAMAGE CONTROL

FOR THE PASTOR'S WIFE

The quick counseling session for pastors,
ministers and missionaries in crisis mode

RICHARD M. SALAZAR JR.

Dedication

To all the "Rambo's" out there who believe it's all about your extraordinary spiritual superpowers! I think it's safe to say that we both know that if it wasn't for God's grace, strength, unwavering fortitude and calling, we would be chasing after the wind. Most of this book was written with tears because I understand the continuous aggression you face from a hell that will not let up until it sees you out on the street wrapped in shame for failing God and the ministry. It's unfair. However, we fight not against flesh and blood but against powers of darkness and spiritual forces of evil in high places. With you in mind, it is because of this, that I wrote this resource. I pray that the words in this book will speak healing, wisdom, and great encouragement to you during those times when it's just you and Satan in the ring. With your Bible, and this book, give him just one more punch and the fight is over!

Introduction

Peter Drucker, the late leadership guru, said that the four hardest jobs in America (and not necessarily in this order) are president of the United States, president of a university, CEO of a hospital, and a pastor. I believe it—I'm a pastor. I grew up as a pastor's kid, and I have planted and pastored my own churches. I have counseled pastors and their families. I also work as an entrepreneur to provide more revenue streams for my family. I know all too well the challenges of leading churches today.

The demands upon a pastor often exceed what they should. The pastor is traditionally considered a church's head "everything." He's the spiritual and administrative head, often the sole minister, the legal corporation president, and the know-it-all, do-it-all, chief cook and bottle washer. In many small churches, he will also conduct all the services, lead all the singing, do all the preaching, and handle all the visitations, counseling, and spiritual matters. He may also have to take care of the office work, bookkeeping, and even the janitorial, maintenance, and building repair.

In my many years in the church, I found many pastors to be some of hardest working, most versatile, multi-skilled people I have ever met. For the main part, they pick up these skills out of the necessity of their circumstances — having no hired staff or few willing volunteers. In too many cases, the pastor has to do far more than he was ever called for or trained to do.

Being a pastor is incredibly difficult. However, this is no excuse to constantly complain about your position. The apostle Paul explains to Timothy that those who aspire to become overseers desire a noble task. We as pastors are called to handle this vocation with the upmost nobility and work hard in our daily tasks while modeling with dutiful and joyful obedience to the Lord the simplicity of the pastoral life. If God has truly called you to ministry, then he will give you the grace, joy, and strength that comes with it.

I have outlined in this book the necessary tools you will need to be the most successful pastor, missionary, or full-time minister you can be. This is a resource that should be used along with the great manual of life, the Bible. Use this resource to find strength and encouragement in all seasons of your ministry life. There is no reason to fail and every reason to be successful as you do the work of a minister!

Table of Contents

Chapter 1

What Makes You Healthy

The health of full-time ministers could be one of the most vital issues we face in the world. The greater the level of their health, the more effective they are at serving their communities and followers with the message of hope, grace, and love. Yet, too often, many God's shepherds act as though the Church fulfills its mission thanks to their own efforts and willpower. When that happens, their health—emotional, spiritual, relational, and physical—suffers.

But remember that Jesus promised that he alone would build his Church. In times of uncertainty, you can take comfort in knowing that everything is not resting on your shoulders. When you pretend you're emotionally healthy and you're not, you are building a house on sand. Jesus said something about that at the end of the Sermon on the Mount. The longer you pretend, the bigger the house gets, and when the storm comes and the sand washes away, the bigger the crash.

Throughout this book, we will talk about the emotional, spiritual, and relational health of full-time pastors and ministers in great detail. But it's important not to overlook physical health in the process. Physical health is crucial to leading too, and God calls us to be good stewards of the bodies he's given us. As we all know, being a pastor can be bad for your health! Pastors have little time for exercise.

Physical health is crucial to leading too, and God calls us to be good stewards of the bodies he's given us.

We often eat meals in the car or at potluck dinners not known for their fresh green salads. The demands on our time are unpredictable and never ending, and our days involve an enormous amount of emotional investment and energy. Exhaustion, poor diet, unmet expectations, and personal isolation would hardly be characteristics of a healthy lifestyle. Yet too often, this accurately describes a hard-working minister of the gospel.

When you combine the fast pace of today's society with the multiple demands of both bio-vocational and full-time ministry, physical health suffers. When that happens, other areas of health tend to suffer, as well. We also set ourselves up for burnout because our bodies don't have what they need to sustain us throughout the day.

Here are three solid tips on staying fit and fresh:

1. Pay attention to what's on your plate.

Eating healthy isn't always easy, but committing to a healthy diet can be one of the smartest decisions you ever make. What you eat has an impact on your brain, including the parts that regulate mood. Although there's no single food that acts as a proven antidepressant, maintaining stable blood sugar through regular, proper nutrition will help you feel better overall on most days.

2. Make time for exercise.

The health benefits of regular exercise and physical activity are hard to ignore. Those benefits are yours for the taking regardless of your age, sex, or physical ability. Exercise can help prevent excess weight gain and helps to promote and maintain weight loss. When you engage in physical activity, you burn calories. The more intense the activity, the more calories you burn. You don't need to set aside large chunks of time for exercise to reap weight-management benefits.

3. Keep an eye on your emotional gauge.

Most of your emotional upsets are caused by lack of harmony, imbalances, and unresolved issues, whether past or present, in the emotional body. Now, here's the kicker. Much of that upset is what you picked up from other people. That's right! You are picking up other people's feelings, thoughts, and emotions all of the time. Your body is an amazing energy-sensing machine and has its own consciousness. It is designed to give you sensory input, but most people don't realize that they're taking on someone else's "junk." As pastors, we are most vulnerable to this since we are interacting 24/7 with people who drag all kinds of emotional baggage with them. We have to careful not to pick it up.

4. Get enough rest.

There is a mistaken notion among many Christians, especially leaders, that without us, the kingdom work might crumble and fall. So what do we do? We neglect rest. I was watching a recent video from a friend who was teaching on this very subject. The sermon was titled "Jesus had a pillow—where's yours?" The main point was that Jesus took time to rest while he was on earth. He understood the urgency of his mission, but he also understood that if he didn't rest, he would quickly burn out.

When Jesus said, "Come to me all you who are weary, I will give you rest" (Matt. 11:28), he meant it. When God rested after creating the universe, he did it for our example, not because he was tired. When God instituted a regimented series of rests for the Israelites, he did it for their own good. God protects us so we can sleep (Psalm 4:8). In order to make that clear, he said: " In vain you rise early and stay up late . . . God grants sleep to those he loves" (Psalm 127:2). It's pretty safe to say that God is for sleep.

FOOD FOR THE SOUL

1 Corinthians 6:19–20

"Or do you not know that your body is a temple of the Holy Spirit within you, whom you have from God? You are not your own, for you were bought with a price. So glorify God in your body."

3 John 1:2

"Beloved, I pray that all may go well with you and that you may be in good health, as it goes well with your soul."

1 Corinthians 3:16–17

"Do you not know that you are God's temple and that God's Spirit dwells in you? If anyone destroys God's temple, God will destroy him. For God's temple is holy, and you are that temple."

Philippians 4:13

"I can do all things through him who strengthens me."

FOOD FOR THOUGHT

"I believe that the greatest gift you can give your family and the world is a healthy you." —Joyce Meyer

"A person whose mind is quiet and satisfied in God is in the pathway to health." — Ellen G. White

"I think that age as a number is not nearly as important as health. You can be in poor health and be pretty miserable at 40 or 50. If you're in good health, you can enjoy things into your 80s." — Bob Barker

DEVOTIONAL

1. Are you trying to make lifestyle changes in your own strength? If so, why? What are some ways you can involve God in making lifestyle changes?

_____

_____

_____

_____

3. Do you agree that happiness is healthiness? Is laughter a kind of medicine?

_____

_____

_____

_____

4. What foods are good for your health? How important is a person's diet to keeping them healthy?

_____

_____

_____

_____

5. Are you getting enough sleep at night? If not, why not? What do you need to do to make sure you do? Do these things starting today!

_____

_____

_____

_____

EXTRA READING

"Five Facets of a Healthy Pastor"

https://www.stewardshipcentral.org/posts/five-facets-of-a-healthy-pastor

"What is it like to be a pastor of a church?"

http://www.victorious.org/cbook/chur30-typical-pastor

"The Secret Pain of Pastors"

http://www.churchleaders.com/pastors/pastor-articles/167379-philip-wagner-secret-pain-of-pastors.html

I also highly recommend purchasing *The Healthy Renegade Pastor: Abandoning Average in Your Health and Wellness* by Nelson Searcy (Church Leader Insights with Nelson Searcy, 2015).

Chapter 2

"It's Lonely Up Here!"

Loneliness is a feeling of emptiness or hollowness inside you. You feel isolated or separated from the world and cut off from those around you, especially those you love and care about.

There are different kinds and degrees of loneliness. You might experience loneliness as a vague feeling that something is not right, or you might experience it as an intense deprivation and deep pain.

Loneliness can be physical or emotional. You might feel lonely because you have some kind of physical separation from others by distance or time. Or you might feel isolated emotionally, even though you are surrounded by people. (Sometimes this is referred to as "feeling alone in a crowd.") As senior pastors, we are around multitudes of people every day, but we often cannot enjoy deeper relationships because we have trust or other issues. We settle for a life of loneliness instead.

Loneliness can become even more intense when you are faced with making a huge decision, especially one you know will be unpopular. You look around for people to turn to, people who know your heart and will support you even if you make a mistake. But don't you know it—people love to hang around you when you're popular and right, but when you are unpopular and controversial, the room is empty.

Every choice we make has a price. The choice to build a support system is no different.

I know this feeling all too well. There are days when I tremble inside and want to go off by myself and cry. There are times when I know I'm going to get pushback from my team so severe that the end result will be despair. Have you ever been there? Have you ever been in a place where you should being receiving the support you need to advance the ministry but found yourself being treated like a criminal instead?

It needs to be emphasized that loneliness is not the same as being alone. A person will always have times when they chose to be alone. Loneliness is the feeling of being isolated and sad about it. All of us feel lonely some of the time. It is only when we feel trapped in our loneliness that it becomes a real problem.

Here are three ways to overcome constant loneliness:

1. Redefine community.

You may look around and wish you were part of a larger community when, in fact, you already are. Or community may be easier to find than you think. Your community doesn't have to be other senior pastors. It could be a men's sports team. It could be a couple of guys from your small group who show up uninvited at 8 AM with a cup of coffee or who pull you away from the computer Monday night to watch the game. By redefining community, sometimes you discover that it's all around you.

2. Build a support system, even at a price.

Every choice we make has a price. The choice to build a support system is no different. It takes an investment of time and resources, and you must build margins into your schedule so you have the time to invest in relationships.

In some cases, this can take as much energy as your career. This can slow down your ministry life a bit, but it can also increase your life satisfaction exponentially. So consider this: What are relationships worth? How much money would it take for you to live a life of solitude? The truth is, no sum is high enough.

3. Take the risk.

Pastors typically have a hard time surrounding themselves with people who will challenge them, build them up, and support them in times of discouragement. But it's important for all of us to have "a few good men" in our lives who have access to us at any time and who are there to encourage us in any way they feel necessary. If you don't have friends like these, find some. Open up. Take risks and allow yourself to be vulnerable. Since loneliness results in isolation, experiment by sharing aspects of yourself, including experiences, feelings, memories, dreams, and desires, with someone you trust. This will help you feel more known and understood.

FOOD FOR THE SOUL

Proverbs 17:17

"A friend loves at all times, and a brother is born for a time of adversity."

Proverbs 27:17

"As iron sharpens iron, so one person sharpens another."

"One who has unreliable friends soon comes to ruin, but there is a friend who sticks closer than a brother."

Ecclesiastes 4:9

"Two are better than one, because they have a good return for their labor. If either of them falls, they help the other up. But pity anyone who falls and has no one to help them up."

FOOD FOR THOUGHT

"While the resurrection promises us a new and perfect life in the future, God loves us too much to leave us alone to contend with the pain, guilt, and loneliness of our present life." — Josh McDowell

"Look for yourself, and you will find in the long run only hatred, loneliness, despair, rage, ruin, and decay. But look for Christ, and you will find him, and with him everything else thrown in." — C. S. Lewis

"The most terrible poverty is loneliness, and the feeling of being unloved." — Mother Teresa

DEVOTIONAL

1. What circumstances cause you to feel lonely?

_____

_____

_____

_____

2. When you are lonely, where do you go or how do you find yourself?

_____

_____

_____

_____

3. Is there any advantage in loneliness? If so, what?

_____

_____

_____

_____

4. What negative thoughts and attitudes do you have that might prevent you from having close relationships with others?

_____

_____

_____

_____

5. What steps can you take right now to begin building relationships that will provide you with the community that you desire? Do you need to redefine community to do that? If so, how?

_____

_____

_____

_____

6. Who are the "few good men" who provide you with friendship and accountability? Write down at least two people who fill these roles. If you haven't already, call them now and invite them into your life. Describe exactly what role you need them to play.

_____

_____

_____

_____

Chapter 3

That's My Line—
Don't Cross It!

Learning to set healthy personal boundaries is necessary for maintaining a positive life. Personal boundaries are the physical, emotional, and mental limits we establish to protect ourselves from being manipulated, used, or violated by others. Boundaries allow us to separate who we are and what we think and feel from the thoughts and feelings of those around us. They are our way of communicating to others that we have self-respect, self-worth, and will not allow others to define us.

The presence of personal boundaries also helps us express ourselves as the unique individuals we are, while we acknowledge the same in others. You must take responsibility for how you allow others to treat you. Your boundaries act as filters for what you will accept in your life and what you will not.

As ministry leaders, we tend to be people pleasers and often put ourselves at a disadvantage by trying to accommodate everyone. We don't want to be selfish, so we put our personal needs on the back burner and agree to do things that may not be beneficial to our well being. You are the highest authority on you. You know yourself best. You know what you need, want, and value. Don't let anyone else make the decisions for you. Healthy boundaries make it possible for you to respect your strengths, abilities, and individuality as well as those of others.

Boundaries aren't just a sign of a healthy relationship. They're a sign of selfrespect.

Below are three keys to building and maintaining better boundaries:

1. Name your limits.

You can't set good boundaries if you're unsure of where you stand. Identify your physical, emotional, and mental limits. Consider what you can tolerate and what makes you feel uncomfortable or stressed. Those feelings help you identify what your limits are.

2. Give yourself permission to have boundaries in the first place.

Fear, guilt and self-doubt are blockades to setting personal boundaries. We might fear the other person's response if we set and enforce our boundaries. We might feel guilty by speaking up or saying no to a family member. We might even wonder if we deserve to have boundaries at all. If you're looking for permission to have boundaries, here it is: Boundaries aren't just a sign of a healthy relationship. They're a sign of self-respect. Give yourself the permission to set boundaries and work to preserve them.

3. Be direct.

With some people, maintaining healthy boundaries doesn't require a direct and clear-cut dialogue. Usually, this is the case with people who are similar to you in their communication styles, views, personalities, and general approach to life. With those who have different personalities or cultural backgrounds, you may need to be more direct.

FOOD FOR THE SOUL

Colossians 4:6

"Let your speech always be gracious, seasoned with salt, so that you may know how you ought to answer each person."

2 Corinthians 6:14

"Do not be unequally yoked with unbelievers. For what partnership has righteousness with lawlessness? Or what fellowship has light with darkness?"

Proverbs 15:1 (KJV)

"A soft answer turneth away wrath: but grievous words stir up anger."

FOOD FOR THOUGHT

"Daring to set boundaries is about having the courage to love ourselves, even when we risk disappointing others." —Unknown author

"Boundaries represent awareness, knowing what the limits are and then respecting those limits." —David W. Earle

"A friend is one that knows you as you are, understands where you have been, accepts what you have become, and still, gently allows you to grow." —William Shakespeare

DEVOTIONAL

1. What do boundaries mean to you and your life?

_____

_____

_____

_____

2. Are you able to set limits and still be a loving person? Why or why not?

_____

_____

_____

_____

3. When you are already pushed to your limits, how are you going to answer the next person who wants your time, love, energy, or money?

_____

_____

_____

_____

4. Are you able to set personal boundaries that protect your **body,** your energy, your time, and your other resources (material, financial, emotional, social) without feeling guilty, fearful, or stressed?

_____

_____

_____

_____

Chapter 4

Protecting Your Wife from the Church

Your spiritual life is weakened by the lifestyle that comes with being the wife of a man whose time is taken up every day by strangers who have captured areas of his heart where you once used to be at the center. - "Damage Control for the Pastor's Wife" written by Richard Salazar Jr.

No pastor's wife should feel this way, but most of them do. Not only does a pastor's wife suffer from her husband's split loyalties, but she struggles with all of the issues you struggle with in the church, including backbiting, being under the microscope, and constant scrutiny and criticism.

Do you have responsibility in this? Yes, you do. Your responsibility is to nurture and protect your wife from these daily realities the best you can. In *1 Corinthians 13 (NIV)*, God tells us that love "always protects." That means more than physical protection. It also means emotional protection, and sometimes, that is even more important. The old saying "Sticks and stones may break my bones but names will never hurt me" just isn't true. Being on the receiving end of emotional pain, including name-calling and emotional abuse, is deeply felt, for certain.

A husband is not only uniquely equipped to protect his family, but it is his biblical responsibility to do so. There is more to doing this than simply being strong and taking the proverbial bullet for your wife. Pastor, you have a responsibility to protect her from the challenges of ministry. You have asked her to be in this position. Now you need to take care of her.

As you already know, the godly husband focuses special attention on protecting his wife. And what man doesn't feel the need to do this? There is something in the very makeup of a man that compels him to protect the woman you love, to shelter her from the pain life can bring.

Here are three crucial areas you need to provide protection for your wife:

1. Protect her emotionally.

The godly husband will protect his wife's heart. One of the ways he does this is by becoming a student of her. He learns what she loves and learns what she hates; he learns what draws her heart to him and what turns her heart from him. He avoids anything that will damage or scar her heart.

2. Protect her spiritually.

Protect your wife spiritually, including your commitment to pray for her and hold her up before the throne of God. Commit yourself to praying for her every day and even many times a day. Pray for her constantly, repeatedly, and unceasingly. Know that as her leader, as her husband, your prayers have special value before God. Tell her that you pray for her and ask her how she would like you to be praying on her behalf. Commit yourself to this practice and look for the evidence of God's response to your earnest supplications.

Boundaries aren't just a sign of a healthy relationship. They're a sign of self respect.

3. Protect her publicly.

Are you protective of your spouse? Do you have her back, even when it creates conflict with others in the church? The partnership of marriage is such that when something or someone hurts or bothers your spouse, it should bother you also. The pain should certainly not be something that is delivered by you. You're "cleaved" together because of marriage. (See *Genesis 2:24; Matthew 19:4–6*.) When you enter this sacred, covenant bond, your hurt becomes her hurt, and her hurt becomes yours.

FOOD FOR YOUR SOUL

1 Peter 3:7

"You husbands in the same way, live with your wives in an understanding way, as with someone weaker, since she is a woman; and show her honor as a fellow heir of the grace of life, so that your prayers will not be hindered."

1 Corinthians 13:7

"Love . . . bears all things, believes all things, hopes all things, endures all things."

1 Corinthians 13:7 (NIV)

"Love protects."

29

"Wives, submit to your husbands, as is fitting in the Lord. Husbands, love your wives, and do not be harsh with them."

FOOD FOR THOUGHT

"Our most basic instinct is not for survival but for family. Most of us would give our own life for the survival of a family member, yet we lead our daily life too often as if we take our family for granted." —Author unknown

"Protect what you love." —Richard M. Salazar, Jr.

"When you love someone, you protect them from the pain. You don't become the cause of it." —Author unknown

DEVOTIONAL

1. Is your wife emotional healthy? If not, do you know why?

_____

_____

_____

_____

2. What is your level of responsibility in your wife's emotional health?

_____

_____

_____

_____

3. Does your weekly routine include learning and protecting your wife's emotions?

_____

_____

_____

_____

4. If one were to ask your wife if you protect her emotions, would she give the same answer as you do? Why or why not?

_____

_____

_____

_____

5. What kinds of things can you do to improve your protection of her emotions?

_____

_____

_____

_____

6. What message can you send to your wife that signals you will do an even better job at this?

_____

_____

_____

_____

Chapter 5

Depression Is Real . . . and It's Nasty

Depression is real, and it is nasty. I speak from experience. I used to suffer from chronic depression, and the worst thing was, I couldn't tell anyone, not even my closest friends. A pastor is supposed to be the rock of his congregation. We're not allowed to be scared or angry or depressed. We're supposed to be filled with joy and positivity all the time. That's nonsense, of course, but it's the perception senior pastors battle.

When I first faced the truth about my chronic depression, I realized the struggle had been with me all of my life. Now I had to learn to cope with it in all of its rawness. People, even my friends and family, would misinterpret my lack of enthusiasm, lack of motivation, and participation and call me names. Lazy, rebellious, and selfish—you name it, I was called it. One day, a pastor friend of mine got me to a place where he could look me in the eye and told me straight up: "Get help!" He told me that my ministry would never get off the ground until I dealt with my emotional issues. Thank God, I listened! I am now free from that depression, and the world looks very different to me. You, too, can have the same fresh start.

When you're depressed, it often feels like nothing in the world can make you feel better.

Anxiety and depression are serious issues. If you are battling with either, the first step is to talk to someone about it. Tell a friend, visit another pastor, or go see a therapist. Don't believe for a moment that you have to fight it alone. Many of the psalmists in God's Word struggled with despair, too. They didn't hunker down and try to ride it out. They were honest about their struggles and turned to God.

Pastors have plenty to make us depressed. Just look at what we deal with on a daily basis: grief, failing marriages, illness, death, drug abuse, poverty, and loss. We deal with other people's financial struggles, not to mention our own. We carry the burdens of our elders, our church members, and the different ministry teams we lead. Oh, yes, and we still need to deliver a stellar message every week even when we, ourselves, are down in the dumps. Then there are the very real needs of our wives and children, whom often feel abandoned as our loyalty is increasingly divided by home and church. The pressure is intense.

Pastors also tend to create lives that are strongly intertwined with their ministries, and their emotional health can become dependent on the state of their ministries. When the ministry is going well, they experience a "high" that comes with success. Conversely, when the ministry is struggling, they can feel like personal failures.

When you're depressed, it often feels like nothing in the world can make you feel better. Depression is devious because the very fact that you are depressed undermines your ability to seek the help that would begin your recovery. Lack of energy, low self-esteem, and dwindling joy in life make it hard to get out of a depressed state.

Here are some steps you can take to counteract the power of depression:

1. Distinguish between emotional and chemical depression.

Some forms of depression are the result of chemical imbalances and require medication. This book is not intended to address this type of depression. Talk to a doctor and determine whether your depression has a chemical component, and if so, address that through your medical care provider.

2. Recognize and counter your critical self-attacks.

Depression is often accompanied by a critical, self-destructive mentality that interferes with and distracts us from our daily lives. When depressed, we tend to accept a negative identity as a true representation of who we are. Many people fail to recognize that this sadistic point of view is actually the voice of our enemy within.

To counteract these negative voices, think of destructive thoughts as being like the parasites that keep you in bed when you're sick. Don't listen to these attacks when they tell you not to pursue your goals, isolate yourself, or forego an activity you enjoy. This gives them even more power over you.

When you notice negative thoughts starting to gain traction over more realistic, positive ways of thinking, it is essential to identify them as an alien point of view. Ask yourself, would you think such cruel thoughts about a friend or family member who was experiencing the same struggles? By having compassion on yourself and recognizing this inner voice as a destructive enemy, you can begin to see who you are more clearly.

3. Think about what could be making you angry.

While some people experience depression as a continual state of sadness or emotional pain, some depression can come in the form of numbness, a lack of feeling that weakens all excitement and smothers the ability to feel joy. Suppressing or cutting off emotions could be a defense against something you aren't comfortable feeling.

Many people who suffer from depression are actually masking feelings of anger and are turning their rage toward someone else or on themselves. If this is you, ask yourself where this anger might be coming from.

Anger can be a hard feeling to accept. From a very young age, we are often told it is bad to be angry. We are told that we need to behave and not to throw tantrums or get into fights (especially when we're children of the ministry). While acting abusive is never acceptable, feeling anger is a natural part of everyday life. By acknowledging and discussing your feelings, you are much less likely to turn your anger against yourself or allow it to lead you into a depressed state.

4. Do things you once liked to do, even if you don't feel like it.

Depression is one of the hardest emotional states to overcome because the symptoms can prevent you from taking the steps you need to get help. It can destroy your will and energy to engage in everyday activities, including those you once loved. Don't give in to lethargy! It will give your depression even more power. Stay active in your life. Pursue those side activities (both inside and outside of ministry) you find of interest. This can help to re-ignite your spark and keep you on your own side.

Though easier said than done, the times you feel most like slumping on the couch are the very ones you should force yourself to take a walk, cook a meal, or call a friend. If you've been depressed in the past, do whatever it was that helped you feel better then. Coping strategies that have worked for you in the past are great places to start. Activities that help you calm down and that raise your spirits are important.

5. Get help.

Seek the help of a qualified professional counselor to provide an outside perspective on your situation and help you develop coping strategies. Sometimes we are so close to a situation that we cannot see a way out, even though someone else clearly can.

FOOD FOR THE SOUL

Philippians 4:8

"Finally, brothers and sisters, whatever is true, whatever is noble, whatever is right, whatever is pure, whatever is lovely, whatever is admirable—if anything is excellent or praiseworthy—think about such things."

Deuteronomy 31:8

"The Lord himself goes before you and will be with you; he will never leave you nor forsake you. Do not be afraid; do not be discouraged."

Psalm 94:17–18

"If the Lord had not helped me, I would have gone quickly to the land of silence. I said, 'I am falling'; but your constant love, O Lord, held me up."

2 Timothy 4:16–17

"No one stood by me the first time I defended myself; all deserted me . . . But the Lord stayed with me and gave me strength."

Isaiah 26:3

"You will keep in perfect peace those whose minds are steadfast, because they trust in you."

FOOD FOR THOUGHT

"Before any great achievement, some measure of depression is very usual." — Charles Spurgeon

"What you believe is very powerful. If you have toxic emotions of fear, guilt, and depression, it is because you have wrong thinking, and you have wrong thinking because of wrong believing." — Joseph Prince

"The deepest fear we have, 'the fear beneath all fears,' is the fear of not measuring up, the fear of judgment. It's this fear that creates the stress and depression of everyday life." —Tullian Tchividjian

DEVOTIONAL

1. What things in your life get you depressed?

_____

_____

_____

_____

2. What negative thoughts and behaviors do you entertain when you are depressed?

_____

_____

_____

_____

3. What benefit do these negative thoughts have for you? Are they undermining your efforts to get help? If so, how?

_____

_____

_____

_____

4. Write down three reasons to talk with someone when you are depressed. Now write down the names of at least two people whom you can call to pray with you when you most need encouragement.

_____

_____

_____

_____

5. Write down three good things going on in your life.

_____

_____

_____

_____

EXTRA READING

"Eight Ways to Actively Fight Depression"

https://www.psychologytoday.com/blog/compassion-matters/201110/eight-ways-actively-fight-depression

Chapter 6

The Lure of the Siren

Pastors have a special role of leadership and power in the church. People look up to them and sometimes view them in god-like terms. Pastors also tend to attract the attention of the women in their congregations.

The reasons are no mystery. Ministers are nice and kind in public, something many husbands are not (either in private or public). Some wives may think the clergyman is better than what they have at home, and a romantic crush may result. Some women are attracted to the aura of power and status. Other times, they are attracted to a pastor's sympathetic kindness. They feel safe around him because surely ministers are godly and never have sexual feelings.

Well, they do. Pastor, you are just like any other man! Intimate relationships do form and can lead to sexual activity. As a pastor, you have free time and can visit homes any time you want, including when husbands are away at work.

41

Paul spoke of this practice by some: "For among them are those who enter into households and captivate weak women weighed down with sins, led on by various impulses" (2 Tim. 3:6). Paul was speaking of bad ministers, but it is a trap that innocent, well-meaning men of God just like you can fall into, as well. Not only are broken church members looking for attention, but so are broken ministers.

> *Sexual sin is everything we entertain with our eyes, our ears, and ultimately, our hearts.*

Ministers spend large amounts of time alone. Many don't have a set schedule or a structured day. They don't have to clock in and out of the office, and they don't usually have church leaders asking them accountability questions. This is especially true for small church ministers who are often the only staff member. Isolation and lack of accountability are seedbeds for disaster.

Sexual temptation breeds deception. This deception is that we can "get away with it," that we can sow without reaping, and that there will be no consequences. However, we must be aware of this insidious lie that the world, the flesh, and the enemy uses to seduce us. A pastor may justify the imaginations of his heart by his past and present pain. He then finds relief through false intimacy on the Internet, or he may actualize his imaginations through sexual encounters with needy women who are looking for a listening ear.

In the end, pastors are deceived into believing that their relational needs will be met and their search for significance will be secured through these activities. Pastor, you will be found out! God guarantees this fact!

Here is something critical for all of us to understand. Affairs don't just happen out of the blue, and sexual sin isn't just hopping into bed with someone who isn't your wife. Sexual sin is everything we entertain with our eyes, our ears, and ultimately, our hearts. Affairs start in the heart, and emotional adultery is every bit as much true adultery as the physical kind. Very often, it's the door that leads to it.

How do we avoid falling into the trap of sexual sin? Jesus was very clear. If your hand sins, cut it off. In other words, if you don't entertain the thought to begin with, it will never have a chance to get a hold on you.

Think of protecting yourself from sexual sin as like pulling weeds in the garden. You pull the weeds out while they are still small, and you pull them out the entire root so they cannot spring back up again. I have a colleague who takes this so seriously that she turns away her eyes when she sees a shirtless man jogging along the street. As a runner herself, it would be easy to convince herself that she's just admiring his physical fitness or his stride. But she knows better. "The heart is deceitful, and wicked above all things." Her love for her husband does not want to compromise the integrity of their intimacy by admiring the body of another man. Her husband, in turn, refuses to meet alone with a woman under any circumstances, even at work. When a colleague comes to his office, he will come to the door and speak to her in the hallway or offer to meet her in a public place. This is the case even if it's someone he and his wife know and consider a family friend.

Temptation is something that can only come in if you open the door. Keep that door shut and locked!

I'm not saying it's easy. Just like you, I have to constantly force my flesh back into obedience. Opportunities to destroy my family and ministry come almost daily, and I have to be aware that I have choices to make every day. Sexual temptation is one of the hardest battles any pastor can face, and victory requires making small, daily choices that make the difference between winning the battle and losing it.

Every day when I turn my computer on, I choose which websites I will view and which I will stay away from. When I grab the remote control to the television, I choose which cable channels I will watch and which I will not. When I am out and about in the community, I choose who to interact with and who not to. If that means choosing the longer line at the bank so I do not interact with the teller with the low-cut neckline, so be it.

The adversary knows your weaknesses and how to play on your emotions. He knows how to get you to rationalize your decisions and compromise in the tiniest ways to keep that door open a crack. The battle is fierce, and it's unrelenting. However, you can win if you purpose in your heart to do so. You will need to take proactive steps every day to keep that door slammed tight. So I ask you, what daily choices do you make in order to win the battle over your flesh?

If you are in the midst of struggling with sexual sin, do the following now!

1. Be honest.

There must be a willingness to confess and confront the issues and facts as they really are. Wrong has to be called wrong, and sin has to be called sin. While sin may be an old term, it's an ever-present reality.

2. Admit you need help.

Someone cannot be helped unless they admit that they need help. You can't dance around the issues. This is no time for games.

3. Make yourself accountable.

Invite into your inner life a few people who love you enough and who are courageous enough to ask you the hard questions. These are people who can tell when you're putting on a front. They won't settle for answers like "Everything is okay" when they know it isn't. Remember, most people will not hold you accountable unless you grant them the right to do so.

Here are five ways you can keep from falling into sexual sin:

1. Think long and hard about the deadly poison of worldly desires.

> "If any one loves the world, the love of the Father is not in him . . . The world passes away, and the lust of it; but he who does the will of God abides for ever" *1 John 2:15,17*

> "Do you not know that friendship with the world is enmity with God? Therefore whoever wishes to be a friend of the world makes himself an enemy of God" *James 4:4*

2. Meditate on the biblical truth that all our acts are acts toward God and not just toward man.

> "The way of the wicked is an abomination unto the Lord: but he loveth him that followeth after righteousness" *Prov. 15:9*

3. Submit yourself to a council of biblically minded, spiritually wise advisers.

> "Without counsel plans go wrong, but with many advisers they succeed" *Prov. 15:22*

4. Give yourself untiringly to the study, meditation, and memorization of Holy Scripture.

> "Strive to present yourself to God as one approved, a workman who has no need to be ashamed, rightly handling the word of truth" *2 Tim. 2:15*

> "On his law he meditates day and night" *Psalm 1:2*

5. Strengthen your marriage.

If something is going on in your marriage that is causing you to feel dissatisfied, fix the problem! Attend a marriage conference. Talk to a professional marriage counselor. Invest in the relationship so that your marriage—and only your marriage—is where you desire to find sexual satisfaction.

"Let your fountain be blessed, and rejoice in the wife of your youth" *Prov. 5:18*

FOOD FOR THE SOUL

James 4:7

"Submit therefore to God. Resist the devil and he will flee from you."

1 Corinthians 6:18–20

"Flee immorality. Every other sin that a man commits is outside the body, but the immoral man sins against his own body. Or do you not know that your body is a temple of the Holy Spirit who is in you, whom you have from God, and that you are not your own? For you have been bought with a price: therefore glorify God in your body."

James 1:12

"Blessed is a man who perseveres under trial; for once he has been approved, he will receive the crown of life which the Lord has promised to those who love him."

FOOD FOR THOUGHT

Quotes from *Finally Free: Fighting for Purity with the Power of Grace* (Heath Lambert, Zondervan 2016):

"Jesus' grace to change you is stronger than pornography's power to destroy you. Jesus' grace is stronger than your own desires to watch sex."

"Until God is your chief concern—until sinning against him is what

46

makes your heart break—you will never turn the corner."

"God does not 'hate' sex; he hates faithless sex with forbidden women, but he loves faithful sexual expressions in the context of marriage. God loves it so much that he commands, not just that it happen, but that it be enjoyed to the point of intoxication."

DEVOTIONAL

1. List all the reasons you might be dissatisfied in your marriage.

_____

_____

_____

_____

2. Which of these reasons are, or would, cause you to look elsewhere for satisfaction?

_____

_____

_____

_____

3. Cyber sex is becoming the most common way a pastor can fulfill his sexual desires outside marriage. If you have ties to online pornography, look up the following Bible verses and identify what sins are associated with the use of Internet pornography or cybersex: *Exodus 20:14, Matthew 5:27–28, Romans 13:13, 1 Peter 2:11, Ephesians 4:25, and Ephesians 5:11–13.* What kind of hurts can Internet relationships cause in a marriage? What kind of hurts outside the marriage?

_____

_____

_____

_____

4. How might problems in a marriage relationship lead to a spouse turning to Internet pornography or cybersex?

_____

_____

_____

_____

5. What can you do starting *today* to eliminate any and all sexual distractions? Be honest about what you can do now and then start doing them *now*.

_____

_____

_____

_____

EXTRA READING

"20 Quotes from 'Finally Free'"

http://www.desiringgod.org/articles/20-quotes-from-finally-free

Chapter 7

Where Did My Time Go?

What is time management? It is a set of principles, practices, skills, and tools that help you use your time wisely. With good time management, leaders of effective churches make certain that their family and work lives are balanced. They make certain that they have time to be missional and about the Great Commission.

If you want to become successful in ministry, you need good timemanagement.

If you want to become successful in ministry, you need good time management. Without these skills, you hand the fate of your day over to chance. You won't steer your life, and you'll eventually do what others want you to do.

Here are a couple of other reasons time management is so important and how it can help you use and manage your time more advantageously:

1. Time is a precious resource that you cannot store or save for later. Everyone has the same amount of time each day. Time not well used cannot be retrieved.

2. Most people feel like they have too much to do and not enough time. They blame lack of time for their poor finances, stress, bad relationships, and not exercising their bodies.

3. By using improved time management skills, you become more productive and can accomplish more with less effort. Time management can help you reduce wasted time and energy, become more creative and productive, and do the right thing at the right time. This will, in turn, lead to better life balance and more fulfillment.

Life presents so many distractions, and it is very easy to lose time on unimportant activities. Ask yourself, what is watching this or that TV program, reading this or that gossip, or participating in a certain activity adding to your life? Is the time spent on a particular activity well spent or just a waste of this precious, finite resource?

FOOD FOR THE SOUL

Ephesians 5:15–17

"Look carefully then how you walk, not as unwise but as wise, making the best use of the time, because the days are evil. Therefore do not be foolish, but understand what the will of the Lord is."

Proverbs 16:9

"The heart of man plans his way, but the Lord establishes his steps."

Proverbs 21:5

"The plans of the diligent lead only to plenty, but everyone who is hasty comes only to poverty."

FOOD FOR THOUGHT

"By failing to prepare, you are preparing to fail." — Benjamin Franklin

"Let our advance worrying become advance thinking and planning." —Winston Churchill

"If you don't know where you are going, you'll end up someplace else." — Yogi Berra

DEVOTIONAL

1. What are your most important goals in life?

_____

_____

_____

_____

2. What activities are scheduled in your daily calendar that help you reach those goals?

_____

_____

_____

_____

4. How long will it take to complete these activities each day? If you need more time to complete them, what are some areas where better time management could help?

_____

_____

_____

_____

5. What are the challenges that prevent you from accomplishing these activities and how can you push past them?

_____

_____

_____

_____

6. Do you need the help of others to get the task done? If so, whom can you ask to help and support you?

_____

_____

_____

_____

Chapter 8

Resisting the Lust for Power

The need for power was identified by the great psychologist David McLelland as one of three largely unconscious drives that motivate people to different degrees. This occurs when you are motivated to dominate and control what other people want, need, or fear in order to get what you want and need and avoid what you fear.

Nowhere can this attitude be found in greater degrees than in the pulpits of churches today. The more power you have, the more power you tend to crave. The desire for power begets the desire for more power. It is a craving that is never satisfied. Few, if any, leaders can survive more than ten years of being power without being tipped into a dangerous and altered state. Most democracies have devised constraints (limited terms of office, for instance) to counteract such dangerous changes to the brain.

Leaders can become intoxicated by power, engaging in wrong behavior simply because they can. Worse of all, they can often get away with it, and their congregations unwittingly enable this behavior by making exceptions for them ("It's okay because he or she is the leader").

The command to "rule" the church is sometimes taken to extremes as well. A pastor's official responsibility is to govern the church in concert with the elders. His focus should be primarily spiritual, attending to matters such as edifying believers and equipping the saints to do the work of the ministry according to *Ephesians 4:12*. However, I have seen too many pastors who are more dictatorial than shepherd-like, requiring those under their authority to seek their permission to an inappropriate degree. Some may require permission even for things unrelated to the ministry, such as making personal investments or going on family vacation. Such men, it seems, simply desire control and are unfit to rule the church of God.

> *The desire for power begets the desire for more power. It is a craving that is never satisfied.*

A pastor's authority originates from God. A pastor does not gain power through seminary graduation, by ordination, or by attending Catalyst training. His authority comes directly from the Holy Trinity. The Father, Son, and Spirit call specific individuals to pastoral ministry.

It is clear from the Scriptures that the apostles were concerned about the danger of developing ecclesiastical bosses. In *2 Corinthians 1:24*, Paul reminds the Corinthians concerning his own apostolic authority: "not that we lord it over your faith; we work with you for your joy." In the same letter he describes, with apparent disapproval, how the Corinthians reacted to certain leaders among themselves: "For you bear it if a man makes slaves of you, or preys upon you, or takes advantage of you, or puts on airs, or strikes you in the face" (*2 Cor. 11:20*). Peter, too, is careful to warn the elders (and he includes himself among them) not to govern by being "domineering over those in your charge, but being examples to the flock." John speaks strongly against Diotrephes "who likes to put himself first, and takes it on himself to put some out of the church." These first-century examples indicate how easily churches then (as today) ignored the words of Jesus: "It shall not be so among you."

Examine the following three ways to help reduce the temptation to control through power:

1. Let go of your ego.

Take yourself down a notch. You're great, but so are others. You have to share the spotlight and let others use their skills. Believe it or not, you're not the best at everything.

2. Get the right people into the right jobs.

One of the most common reasons leaders micromanage or take on controlling tendencies is because they are afraid to hand the reigns over to their team members. Sometimes it isn't that they don't want to relinquish power, but that they don't trust the capabilities or judgment of those around them. When you empower your people, you must also learn to let go.

3. Acknowledge that you can't control everything.

Give yourself a break and learn to go with the flow now and again. Once you see everything works out just fine without your intervention, you'll get more comfortable with the idea.

FOOD FOR THE SOUL

Philippians 2:3–4 (AMP)

"Do nothing from selfishness or empty conceit [through factional motives, or strife], but with [an attitude of] humility [being neither arrogant nor self-righteous], regard others as more important than yourselves. Do not merely look out for your own personal interests, but also for the interests of others."

1 John 4:18

"There is no fear in love, but perfect love casts out fear. For fear has to do with punishment, and whoever fears has not been perfected in love."

1 Peter 5:7

"Cast all your anxiety on him because he cares for you."

FOOD FOR THOUGHT

"Anywhere, anytime ordinary people are given the chance to choose, the choice is the same: freedom, not tyranny; democracy, not dictatorship; the rule of law, not the rule of the secret police." —Tony Blair

"Stop obeying a dictator; you will then see that he is nothing! Stop obeying an earthly king; you will then see that he is nothing! If you refuse the Devil, you will then see that he will fade away!" — Unknown author

DEVOTIONAL

1. Do you feel the need to be in control of everything? If so, what's the real motivation behind it?

_____

_____

_____

_____

2. Do you really have a servant's heart or are your efforts really disguised attempts to control others?

_____

_____

_____

_____

3. Do you lead by example or do you expect others to tow the line and do as you say?

_____

_____

_____

_____

4. Do you blast people when they violate the smallest rule of your list ("Do as I say, not as I do")? If so, what motivates that attitude?

_____

_____

_____

_____

5. Who's really in control of your life? Have you truly surrendered it to God or do you have purple knuckles from gripping the wheel so hard?

_____

_____

_____

_____

EXTRA READING

"Too Much Power Can Do Very Odd Things to a Leader's Head"

http://theconversation.com/too-much-power-can-do-very-odd-things-to-a-leaders-head-23945

Chapter 9

Family First, Ministry Second

What is the biggest lie any pastor can buy into? Ministry first, family second. Maybe you have not yet fallen for this lie, or maybe you're living it right now. Either way, even if you're not already seeing the negative effects of this falsehood, you soon will. Even the best pastors have at some point lived this lie and repented after experiencing devastating results. Let's look at a few of them.

In his sunset years, Billy Graham was asked about any regrets in life. His first answer was that he had not spent enough time with his family.[1]

R. T. Kendal, the most recent pastor to lead Westminster Tabernacle (the great church founded by C. H. Spurgeon in London), was once asked what he regretted most in life. His answer was that he did not spend enough time with his children.[2]

1   https://billygraham.org/story/notable-quotes-from-billy-graham/

2   http://www.rejoicebookstoreonline.com/item/r-t-kendall/in-pursuit-of-his-glory/8194.html

More recent is the divorce and remarriage of Benny and Suzanne Hinn. They both agree that Benny's lack of time for his family caused the breakdown in the marriage.[3]

Billy Graham, R. T. Kendal, and Benny Hinn are notable figures within the body of Christ, and all three had the same regret—not spending time with family because they mistakenly thought ministry should come first.

> *There are countless pastors whose homes are broken because they put ministry before family.*

There are countless pastors whose homes are broken because they put ministry before family. Now their children want nothing to do with God or the ministry, and there is great resentment that invades these homes. Nothing good comes when a pastor leaves his family behind. Ministry is hard enough without the added stress of issues at home. Many ministry leaders have real trouble in their families that gets ignored, relegated, or forgotten. You can think you can hide these problems, but private conflicts almost always come back to affect you publicly, usually at the worst possible time. Secret monsters damage public ministry.

While there has been growing discussion about the impact of ministry on pastors' marriages, the impact on their children is too often overlooked. Among the very serious issues faced by pastors' kids are struggles with identity, depression and substance abuse, inability to trust, and discouragement. Instead of raising children who embrace their relationships with God, they raise children who abandon them. The challenges of pastors' wives are much the same: uncertain identity, inability to trust and form meaningful relationships, scars from backbiting and constant criticism, and loneliness and resentment. Many have pain so deep that they succumb to substance abuse and infidelity. All of these things are preventable, and while your wife and children carry their own responsibilities in them, as the leader of your home, you need to do everything you can to protect them.

(If you or members of your family are looking for resources to help, you can check out my two other books, *Hey! Where's My Chicken Soup! Remembering the Forgotten "Soul" of the Preacher's Kid and Damage Control for the Pastor's Wife.*)

But what about your ministry? You can't leave that behind, can you? Pastor, your family is your ministry! That does not mean you become lazy or forget that you also have a job, but in the rare case that you have to choose, you choose family. Our wives and children are with us for a short time, so we must make the sacrifice to care for them. Yes, ministry takes time too, but I have found that if you choose the important, God takes care of the urgent. Here's a fact that may help you find the balance—the moment you decide to be a real father and husband, your church will grow more! You won't regret the extra time you spend with your wife and children.

Here are four reasons family time rocks:

1. It builds self-esteem in children.

Children who spend time with their parents and participate in activities together build a positive sense of self-worth. When children feel valued by their parents, they feel more positive about themselves. Family activities don't have to be expensive or luxurious to be meaningful. Take a walk together, go for a bike ride, or play a game of basketball in the driveway. The important part is just being together and enjoying each other's company.

2. It strengthens family bonds.

Families who share everyday activities (including vacations and daily excursions) form strong emotional ties. A study published in the journal "Family Relations" found that families that enjoy group activities share stronger emotional bonds as well as the ability to adapt well to life's challenging circumstances . . . together.

3. It creates happy memories.

Family time creates warm memories for parents and children alike. Children with happy family memories are more likely to create loving environments for their own children when they grow up. Learning to work and play as a family is one of the best lessons children can be taught so they can develop into competent adults and parents.

4. It helps parents and children reconnect.

Spending time together helps busy parents reconnect with their children. Children tend to share more information about their lives while enjoying an activity together than when asked, "What did you do today?" It is also a time when life lessons like sharing, fairness, and compassion can be reinforced without conflict. Children grow and change quickly, so family time is a wonderful time to get to know your children better.

FOOD FOR THE SOUL

1 Corinthians 13:4–7

"Love is patient and kind; love does not envy or boast; it is not arrogant or rude. It does not insist on its own way; it is not irritable or resentful; it does not rejoice at wrongdoing, but rejoices with the truth. Love bears all things, believes all things, hopes all things, endures all things."

It takes love, patience, and endurance to make time for family.

"But if anyone does not provide for his relatives, and especially for members of his household, he has denied the faith and is worse than an unbeliever."

Your time is the best thing you can provide for your family. It will last a lifetime!

"Train up a child in the way he should go; even when he is old he will not depart from it."

Giving of your time for your family will influence your children in ways you might never know. Just do it!

FOOD FOR THOUGHT

"A man should never neglect his family for business." — Walt Disney

"Love your family. Spend time, be kind and serve one another. Make no room for regrets. Tomorrow is not promised and today is short." — Author unknown

"Family is the most important thing in the world." — Princess Diana

DEVOTIONAL

1. Get your family around the kitchen table and ask them if you're spending enough time with them. Then sit back and listen. Don't interrupt or speak back into what they are saying. Just listen. You might be surprised by what you hear. Summarize what they tell you here.

_____

_____

_____

_____

2. Do you regularly spend more time at the office than you do with your family? If so, why? Do your reasons justify neglecting family time?

_____

_____

_____

_____

3. Take an honest assessment of your family. Do you see any signs of dysfunctionality? If so, is it because they are not feeling sufficient leadership from you? (This includes spending time with them and not just dishing out orders.)

_____

_____

_____

_____

4. Your family needs to feel you are there for them. Not just by word, but in action. What can you do right now to start planning a family vacation, or if you cannot take an extended break, at least a day out with your family?

_____

_____

_____

_____

5. What steps can you take to make sure time with family is on your weekly calendar?

_____

_____

_____

_____

Chapter 10

Whom Can I Trust?

Do you trust the people on your team? It's an uncomfortable question to ask. As good leaders, we work hard to create a supportive environment and earn the trust of the people who follow us.

Pastors always face a dilemma in seeking to trust those around them. This includes both congregants and staff. Because of the revolving door that often comes with pastoring a church, there will always be those whom you think are behind your efforts no matter what, then they walk out when you least expect it. It just comes with the territory. As a result, many pastors tend to build an emotional wall, keeping themselves distant from others. Building a wall might keep from getting hurt, but it also keeps you from effectively ministering and loving those around you.

Being able to trust your staff is hard enough when things in the church are going well. It becomes even more challenging in the midst of chaos. The reason most churchgoers distrust leadership in general is because they have had a bad experience. As a leader, most likely you already know what to do to win the hearts and minds of those you lead. There are also several resources in the marketplace to help. However, there are not as many tools to help you deal with your distrust of people themselves, which can ultimately bring hurt to both sides.

As pastors, the question we need to ask ourselves is, "Are we fully engaged with others?" If you are finding yourself increasingly disengaged, ask yourself what has caused you, first, to distrust people and, second, disengage from them? Whatever your answer, is it a valid reason for you to build emotional walls? Such walls send signals to your congregation that they must keep their distance. This is the very opposite of a compassionate leader. Jesus had fastballs thrown at him every day, but he remained engaged and compassionate because he was able to keep the long game at the forefront of everything that he did.

If you practice what you preach, you will have followers for a lifetime. It is that simple.

Engagement is often viewed as a "management thing" rather than a "ministry thing." Yet it is even more important for pastors than business leaders. It is critical to engage your congregations day to day, yet many pastors do not realize how their engagement (or lack thereof) affects their church's performance and productivity.

Here are five things you can do to help take a sledgehammer to that wall of distrust:

1. Practice what you preach.

If you practice what you preach, you will have followers for a lifetime. It is that simple. People aren't looking to push your buttons. They just want sincerity in all you do for them.

2. Listen, listen, listen!

Pastors are good at preaching to people, but many don't know how to listen. Your job isn't just to preach well. It's also to listen well. You need to hear people's needs and concerns. Churches grow because pastors choose to listen and then help solve "people issues."

3. Don't be a people pleaser.

Many pastors feel like failures because they can't please everyone. This is a trap. You might be able to please everyone for a short time, but you cannot do this indefinitely. Nobody can. When you burn out trying to accomplish pleasing everyone, it often backfires. Their trust is lost and, in turn, you build a wall of distrust.

FOOD FOR THE SOUL

1 Corinthians 13:4–7

"Love is patient, love is kind and is not jealous; love does not brag and is not arrogant, does not act unbecomingly; it does not seek its own, is not provoked, does not take into account a wrong suffered, does not rejoice in unrighteousness, but rejoices with the truth; bears all things, believes all things, hopes all things, endures all things."

1 Corinthians 11:17–19

"But in giving this instruction, I do not praise you, because you come together not for the better but for the worse. For, in the first place, when you come together as a church, I hear that divisions exist among you; and in part I believe it. For there must also be factions among you, so that those who are approved may become evident among you."

Psalm 37:3

"Trust in the Lord and do what is right! Settle in the land and maintain your integrity!"

FOOD FOR THOUGHT

"Trust is the first step to love." —Author unknown

"Learning to trust is one of life's most difficult tasks." —Isaac Watts

"He who does not trust enough, will not be trusted." — Author unknown

DEVOTIONAL

1. You truly trust your congregation and staff? Why or why not?

_____

_____

_____

_____

2. What issues are causing you to feel this way?

_____

_____

_____

_____

3. How can you work to resolve these issues and break free from the entrapment created by your own barriers?

_____

_____

_____

_____

4. When people know you trust them, they tend to rise to the occasion. What steps can you take to show others that you genuinely trust them?

_____

_____

_____

_____

5. Trusting doesn't mean you have to trust everyone, but you do need to have some faith in your congregation. List the people you can trust in key positions that allow you to confidently move forward in your ministry.

_____

_____

_____

_____

Chapter 11

Is Cultural Relevance All It's Cracked Up to Be?

I've seen too many pastors quit the ministry, become depressed, and mismanage finances because they tried to become what everyone else is trying to do—be relevant! I have friends who, even as I write this book, are discouraged because their efforts to become relevant in modern culture are not working.

This issue was recently driven home by a woman who contacted me, desperate to reach her wayward son. "I don't want to offend him," she lamented. "I don't want him to think I'm irrelevant because I believe the Bible!" She went on to say she was even more confused about how to reach her son because her pastor was unwilling to address cultural issues that affect his faith. On one hand, she understands that we need to be careful not to "push anyone away." Yet her pastor's passive stance on issues that her family is facing confused her. Her struggle deepened. After all, what good mother would push her son away with "Bible verses 'n stuff"? This sounds a little "yesterday," and "churchy" in today's progressive culture, don't you think?

> *There is no greater attraction than working signs, wonders, and miracles in the public arena.*

But is it? I might be alone here, but I think our struggle for cultural relevance is robbing the Church of the one thing that actually makes us relevant. We can draw a crowd with our hipster services and "feel good" gospel, but tell me, how's that working for us?

The goal in these pages is not to force a specific theological perspective down your throat. It is to guide you into finding what brings life back into your spirit. However, please indulge me as I divert from that approach for a second. Jesus left pastors a pattern to follow if we are to be successful in ministry. Being "relevant" isn't part of it. In fact, Jesus defined what would be relevant for all times, and he commissioned the church to be exactly that. What is it? It is to be miracle workers! There is no greater attraction than working signs, wonders, and miracles in the public arena. If you feel like relevancy hasn't worked for you, get back to the basics!

Michael Brown recently wrote in "Charisma" magazine:

Let us always be careful not to put relevance before obedience and not to water down the Word in order to avoid offense. Put another way, we must not use the shifting tides of culture and the fickle opinions of people as our guide for life and ministry. Instead, we must seek to emulate Jesus in thought, word and deed, lifting Him up without shame (which includes lifting up His life-giving standards of holiness and purity). If we do, the hungry and thirsty will come.[4]

Likewise, Kris Valloton of KV Ministries recently wrote on Facebook:

We are not called to reflect our culture. We are called to transform it. Becoming darkness to be relevant to a world of immorality is not the pathway to progress, but the process to the cesspool of hopelessness. We must lovingly reach into the cesspool of society and dirty our hands with the souls of men as we pull them into the light of His extravagant grace.[5]

This doesn't mean that we shouldn't try to reach out in culturally relevant ways to try to draw in younger audiences. Many churches are adding contemporary music, incorporating Spanish-language services, and using culturally relevant staging to appeal to younger audiences. These are good things, but it's important not to get too caught up in them so that you are judging yourself by how well they are received.

Here are two ways to overcome the "relevant" heartache:

1. Remember who you are.

Comparing yourself to the world's "bells and whistles" can become a habit that is hard to break. You'll often find yourself measuring yourself up to the latest gimmicks before you even realize it, but that doesn't mean you have to continue doing it. When you find yourself getting trapped in the "relevancy" game, remind yourself who you are in Christ. As a pastor, you are called to lead people into a life of true relevancy—living and sharing the miraculous!

2. Check your pride meter.

Often times, pastors feel that, if their presentation isn't culturally relevant, they are of lesser importance. Their pride keeps them wasting money, time, and energy on trying to make their appearances attractive to the outsider. Comparing ourselves to what's culturally relevant can bring feelings of superiority that cause us to feel prideful.

---

5   https://www.facebook.com/kvministries/posts/10152439908303741

In comparing ourselves to culture, we will most likely feel superior in some areas where others are weak. Proverbs 16:18 says, "Pride goes before destruction, and a haughty spirit before a fall." If left unaddressed, our tendency to compare ourselves to others can lead to an arrogant mindset from which it is very difficult to break free.

FOOD FOR THE SOUL

1 Corinthians 1:22–24

"For Jews demand signs and Greeks seek wisdom, but we preach Christ crucified, a stumbling block to Jews and folly to Gentiles, but to those who are called, both Jews and Greeks, Christ the power of God and the wisdom of God."

1 Corinthians 2:4

"My message and my preaching were not in persuasive words of wisdom, but in demonstration of the Spirit and of power."

1 Thessalonians 4:1

"Finally then, brethren, we request and exhort you in the Lord Jesus, that as you received from us instruction as to how you ought to walk and please God (just as you actually do walk), that you excel still more."

FOOD FOR THOUGHT

"If Jesus Christ was who he claimed to be, and he did die on a cross at a point of time in history, then, for all history past and all history future it is relevant because that is the very focal point for forgiveness and redemption." —Josh McDowell

"To be a Christian who is willing to travel with Christ on his downward road requires being willing to detach oneself constantly from any need to be relevant, and to trust ever more deeply the Word of God." —Henri Nouwen

"The thing that alarms me is that there are so many clergymen who say that the so-called 'new morality' is all right. They say we're living in a new generation; let's be relevant, let's change God's law. Let's say that adultery is all right under certain circumstances; fornication's all right under certain circumstances. If it's 'meaningful.'" — Billy Graham

"A church in retreat doesn't give answers. It doesn't storm the gates of hell. It settles and makes peace where there is no peace." — Andrew Walker

DEVOTIONAL:

1. What reasons are driving you to be overly concerned with cultural relevancy?

_____

_____

_____

_____

2. Do these reasons align with Scripture? If not, are you willing to rethink your positions?

_____

_____

_____

_____

3. What areas of your church are overtaken by relevancy? Have these areas produced fruit according to Scripture?

_____

_____

_____

_____

4. Have you spent more money trying to be culturally relevant than you have on missions for the year? If so, what is the Holy Spirit saying to you about this issue?

_____

_____

_____

_____

Chapter 12

If It Feels Good . . . The Lure of Substance Abuse

Do pastors wrestle with addictions? Of course they do. Addictions are a growing threat to congregations and those in ministry. Some pastors and denominations are just starting to openly address this problem, while others have been trying to solve it quietly for a long time. Whether a pastor is dealing with a member of his congregation or wrestling with his own personal problem, the threat is very real and dangerous.

Pastors are not immune to any form of addiction, including pornographic addiction, food addiction, prescription drug addiction, drug addiction, gambling, and workaholicism.

Let's consider these statistics:

* 4 in 10 pastors view pornography daily.

- Food addition and obesity is the number one health problem for ministers.

- Abuse of illegal and prescription drugs, along with gambling, are escalating as ways of escape.

- 90% of pastors are workaholics. They burn a candle at both ends and work between 55–75 hours weekly.[6]

As pastors confront their addictions and escapist behaviors, they face the dilemma of disclosure. Whom can they talk to? Whom can they find today to help them begin the healing process? Pastor, only you can decide to make the turnaround as quickly and as painlessly as possible. That takes guts. It takes time, commitment, and dedication to see the deliverance process through.

Pastors are not immune to any form of addiction...

One of the realities of addictive behaviors is that honesty and integrity are the first casualties. Those affected by addiction quickly master the art of deception. They become good at hiding their behavior, masking it behind denial, half-truths, and well-covered tracks. They preserve the false assumptions others have about them. Addicts are extraordinarily adept at denial, manipulation, rationalization, and justification. A plethora of defense mechanisms are at work inside the addict. It has been said that addicts live in two diametrically opposed worlds. They are desperately looking for help while taking drastic measures to protect their addiction.

As long as the addictive or compulsive behavior is being indulged, it is unlikely that the individual will reach out for the help they need, even if they want it. The first step, therefore, must be a total break with the behavior. Formal treatment in an inpatient or outpatient setting may be necessary. You, pastor, must choose this first step.

At an absolute minimum, the pastor struggling with addiction must discontinue the behavior, repent, and become rigorously honest with his or her spouse and possibly other family members. He must establish an accountability relationship with at least one other individual. This accountability partner cannot be a subordinate. It must be someone outside the ministry and preferably a trusted friend or colleague who has either been through the process personally or who has adequate training in the area of concern. This is an individual who cannot be manipulated. Many addicts want recovery on their own terms. It doesn't work!

If you struggle with any kind of addictive behavior, the following are three things you need to start implementing now:

1. Find accountability. Without accountability and a caring, supportive network, isolation lends itself to obtaining "things of pleasure." This may include sex, food, drugs, or something else. Pastor, you are too important to be left alone, allowing the temptations of this world to deceive and destroy you, your family, and your ministry.

2. Rid yourself of guilt and shame. Too many pastors struggle with guilt and shame just by being tempted. Don't let guilt paralyze you. Even Jesus was tempted in the wilderness, but he overcame through the Word and through his relationship with his Father.

3. Stay connected to God daily. Everyone must maintain that relationship with Abba Father on a daily basis. You must recognize your weaknesses and from where you get our strength.

FOOD FOR THE SOUL

1 Corinthians 10:13

"No temptation has overtaken you but such as is common to man; and God is faithful, who will not allow you to be tempted beyond what you are able, but with the temptation will provide the way of escape also, so that you will be able to endure it."

1 Corinthians 15:33

"Do not be deceived: 'Bad company corrupts good morals.'"

James 4:7

"Submit yourselves, then, to God. Resist the devil, and he will flee from you."

FOOD FOR THOUGHT

"If Jesus Christ was who he claimed to be, and he did die on a cross at a point of time in history, then, for all history past and all history future it is relevant because that is the very focal point for forgiveness and redemption." —Josh McDowell

"To be a Christian who is willing to travel with Christ on his downward road requires being willing to detach oneself constantly from any need to be relevant, and to trust ever more deeply the Word of God." —Henri Nouwen

"The thing that alarms me is that there are so many clergymen who say that the so-called 'new morality' is all right. They say we're living in a new generation; let's be relevant, let's change God's law. Let's say that adultery is all right under certain circumstances; fornication's all right under certain circumstances. If it's 'meaningful.'" — Billy Graham

"A church in retreat doesn't give answers. It doesn't storm the gates of hell. It settles and makes peace where there is no peace." — Andrew Walker

DEVOTIONAL

1. Take an honest assessment of your life and write down the addictions that are destroying your health, family, and ministry.

_____

_____

_____

_____

2. Now that you have identified your addictions, are you willing to speak with your spouse about them so that you can come up with a path toward deliverance together? If not, why not? There should be no excuse to not speak with your spouse. Healing can be painful for both parties, but going through the process together will help you find freedom faster.

_____

_____

_____

_____

3. Once you both are aware and in agreement that you are going to get help, do it! Use this time to research and find the right relationships and counselors to help you start your journey toward recovery. Don't wait! Do it now!

_____

_____

_____

_____

EXTRA READING

"The Transparent Pastor: When a Pastor Struggles with an Addiction, Who Needs to Know?"

http://www.christianitytoday.com/pastors/2009/spring/
whenapastorstruggles.html

Chapter 13

Putting Money in Its Place

Larry Burkett, noted financial author, says, "Money is either the best or the worst area of communication in our marriages."[7]

As a pastor and counselor who has worked with many married couples, I can personally vouch for the fact that money is the thing couples fight about the most. It is also one of the major causes of divorce. The homes of pastors are no exception. A poll conducted by Grey Matter Research in July 2015, found the following:

*   90% of pastors feel some level of financial stress in their families and church work.

*   76% of pastors know other pastors who left the ministry due to financial pressures.

*   63% of pastors' spouses work outside the home.

*   31% of pastors work a second job to help make ends meet.

- Around 60% of pastors do not receive health insurance or retirement funds from their church.

- 25% of pastors have medical bills averaging $7,253.

- Over 80% of pastors serve congregations in rural and smaller communities. Only 19% serve in a large city or large city suburb.

- Over half of pastors have served their current congregations for more than six years. [8]

So pastor, if you and your spouse have fights over money, you are normal. Our family struggles with budgeting, staying on budget, and general spending, too. (So I'm not speaking from an ivory tower here.) I, myself, struggle with running multiple ministries, running personal businesses, and raising a family just like you do. So think of this as an opportunity to work together. Instead of allowing your finances to destroy you, allow your finances to be an opportunity to find areas of agreement. I'm not talking about agreement brought on by surrender, but rather by understanding the other's view, each person getting a vote, and finding common ground. "Submit one to another out of reverence for Christ" (*Eph. 5:21 NIV*).

> *Instead of allowing your finances to destroy you, allow your finances to be an opportunity to find areas of agreement.*

Face it, if you and your wife can agree on the checkbook, there would be little left to fight about except who has the remote. This doesn't mean that you'll always see things the same way. Men tend to take more financial risks and not to save for emergencies. They use money as a scorecard and can struggle with self-esteem when there are financial problems. Women tend to see money more for its perceived security, so they gravitate toward investing in the rainy-day fund. They can have a level of fear (my wife, Sharon, calls it "terror") when money problems arise. Men and women are different in how they view money, and it is largely because they process problems and opportunities from different vantage points.

All of this becomes exacerbated in an environment in which there is little money to go around. This is a common problem, especially in smaller churches where pastors do not receive high salaries and often have to work a second job to make ends meet. In these situations, the pastor's wife may need to take a job to help with the family finances. If the elders, the congregation, and other ministry leaders expect your wife to be an integral part of the ministry, this may require you to set new expectations about what she will and will not be able to do. She needs to be given the freedom to work part-time (or full-time, if necessary) without being made to feel guilty about it.

Here are three ways to get your finances under control:

1. Create a family budget.

When you are working on a limited budget, identify where your money is going, then create a budget to ensure that it is being spent wisely. How much do you typically spend on food? Utilities? Clothing and other necessities? After all of the bills have been paid, how much money is left over and how is it being spent? Creating a family budget and agreeing on discretionary spending is the first step toward financial security.

2. Draw a line between personal finances and ministry.

Especially in small churches, it can be easy to cross the line between your personal funds and the church funds. On one hand, pastors can feel pressured to "over give" into building and other ministry funds if they fall short, creating pressure on their own finances. On the other hand, it can be easy to "borrow" from the church funds to pay bills when your own funds are tight. Consider having someone else keep the financial records for your home and ministry to avoid conflicts and temptation.

3. Give your wife the freedom to work, if necessary.

In an ideal world, your wife would be able to devote her full time and attention to your family and ministry if she desires to do so. But in some cases, there may be no other option. Whether she takes a job outside the home or starts a home-based business, support her efforts and tell her that you're grateful for her willingness to sacrifice her time for the sake of your family.

FOOD FOR THE SOUL

Proverbs 3:9–10 (NASB)

"Honor the Lord from your wealth and from the first of all your produce; so your barns will be filled with plenty and your vats will overflow with new wine."

2 Corinthians 9:6–8 (NASB)

"Now this I say, he who sows sparingly will also reap sparingly, and he who sows bountifully will also reap bountifully. Each one must do just as he has purposed in his heart, not grudgingly or under compulsion, for God loves a cheerful giver. And God is able to make all grace abound to you, so that always having all sufficiency in everything, you may have an abundance for every good deed."

Proverbs 13:22 (NASB)

"A good man leaves an inheritance to his children's children, and the wealth of the sinner is stored up for the righteous."

FOOD FOR THOUGHT

"Any sensible family has a budget that lays out how much will be spent for household and other purposes. Without such planning, things would quickly go awry." —Walter Ulbricht

"Some couples go over their budgets very carefully every month; others just go over them." —Sally Poplin

"I have enough money to last me the rest of my life, unless I buy something." —Jackie Mason

DEVOTIONAL

1. Have you and your wife worked together to create a family budget? Do you agree on the details of the budget, or at least have you agreed to support one another in the areas where you disagree?

_____

_____

_____

_____

2. Does your family budget include giving back to God his rightful portion of your finances?

_____

_____

_____

_____

3. If you do not have a family budget, what keeps you from creating one? Are you afraid to take an honest look at your finances? What do you need to do to make that happen?

_____

_____

_____

_____

3. Most of us have areas where we could spend more wisely. What are the areas of your life that need serious cuts in spending?

_____

_____

_____

_____

4. Do you think that your spending priorities fall in line with God's? Why or why not? How do you think God wants you to prioritize your spending?

_____

_____

_____

_____

Chapter 14

Ignoring Sound Advice

This may sound overly basic, but our lives often turn on the basics. In fact, do you realize how many pastors are either out of the ministry or struggling because of one piece of advice they either intentionally ignored (or didn't seek clarification on) and it ended up going in one ear and out the other? There are so many missing God's best because they are not listening to him directly or because he is using others to speak into their lives and they are not willing to listen.

Pastors are good at dishing it out, but terrible at taking it in. What do I mean by that? When it comes time for us to receive guidance, direction, or correction, we usually just let it float on by without realizing God is trying to throw us a lifeline. I have the privilege of being invited into the homes of pastors, missionaries, and ministers to provide guidance and perspective on a daily basis. If there one underlying pattern in many of these families, it is that somewhere along the way, they did not heed to sound advice. When they are struggling and I start to probe about the turning points in their lives that got them this point, it never fails that they can think back to when sound advice was given and they did not heed it.

Pastors need to realize is that there is a time to preach, but there's also a time to hear. Unfortunately, most are more inclined to give it than to take it. There is a reason that people say, "God gave us two ears and one mouth!" What is it that keeps us from being better listeners? In a word, it's pride. We love ourselves—along with what we say, think, and do—more than we love other people. As painful as it may be to hear, pride is the sinful barrier that often keeps us from listening to others. Pride is like cancer. It is a vicious and malignant sin, yet it has a whole variety of manifestations.

> *When it comes time for us to receive guidance, direction, or correction, we usually just let it float on by without realizing God is trying to throw us a lifeline.*

Pastors get stuck in the preaching rut. Even when we're not preaching, we're preaching. Personal conversations, counseling sessions, and even family devotions can easily morph into Sunday-style sermonizing, even if by sheer habit. Preaching, as necessary and life changing as it is, can actually be the pastor's weakness, especially if it's done to the neglect of active, intentional, and careful listening. Listening is a lost Christian trait, and sadly, it's pastors and church leaders who have been some of the first casualties. Leadership, counseling, and preaching must include being willing to listen.

For many, the advice you are offered can be a "make or break" deal. So, listen up! No matter what it is, and no matter what area of life or ministry, be in constant listening mode. You never know when your spirit will pick up something that you need to hear. It might come from a minister, a member of your staff, or a member of your church. It might be someone on the street or even the barista as you order a cup of coffee. Just remember, God can (and will) use anyone and anything to speak to you.

FOOD FOR THE SOUL

Proverbs 12:15

"The way of a fool is right in his own eyes, but a wise man listens to advice."

Proverbs 11:14

"Where there is no guidance, a people falls, but in an abundance of counselors there is safety."

Proverbs 19:20–21

"Listen to advice and accept instruction, that you may gain wisdom in the future. Many are the plans in the mind of a man, but it is the purpose of the Lord that will stand."

FOOD FOR THOUGHT

"Wisdom is the reward you get for a lifetime of listening when you'd have preferred to talk." — Doug Larson

"Courage is what it takes to stand up and speak; courage is also what it takes to sit down and listen." — Winston Churchill

"Big egos have little ears." — Robert H. Schuller

DEVOTIONALS

1. Are you a regular listener to sound advice? If not why not?

_____

_____

_____

_____

2. What can you do to be aware of good counsel throughout your day?

_____

_____

_____

_____

3. Are you afraid of implementing sound advice? If so, why?

_____

_____

_____

_____

4. Think back and ask God to remind you of times that you missed solid advice. Write down those times and the advice that you ignored, then write down an action plan to prevent this from happening again.

_____

_____

_____

_____

EXTRA READING

"Leadership Skills Are Listening Skills: How Learning to Listen Improves Your Pastoral Counseling"

http://www.sharefaith.com/blog/2010/11/leadership-skills-listening-skills-learning-listen-improves-pastoral-counseling/

Chapter 15

Battling Burnout

As I was coming to the end of writing this book, I started to feel a sense of burnout. When it came to making changes, adding content, or enduring the editing process, I just couldn't bring myself to focus the way the demands of this book needed me to. My "A" game went to an "F" game within hours. These are issues I'm passionate about. Shouldn't I be overflowing with ideas? Yet I found myself clueless and worn out. That evening, a video link showed up in my inbox of a pastor of a megachurch announcing his resignation due to . . . *burnout*!

Suddenly, I was reminded of why I'm running this race. My heart was broken for this man because of his state of mind and spirit, but also because of the short and long-term damage it will do to his congregation. Announcements like this almost always come with some sort of transitional pain. But this pain is inevitable. Burnout is a real problem, and for pastors, it is a real threat to you, your family, your ministry, and your church. According to one study, moral failure is only the second most common reason pastors leave the ministry.[9] The first is burnout.

If constant stress has you feeling disillusioned, helpless, and exhausted, you may be suffering from burnout. When you're feeling this way, problems seem insurmountable. Everything looks bleak, and it's difficult to muster up the energy to care, let alone do something about it. The unhappiness and detachment that burnout causes can threaten your ministry, your relationships, and your health.

Burnout reduces productivity and saps your energy. It leaves you feeling helpless, hopeless, cynical, and resentful. Eventually, you may feel like you have nothing more to give. Most of us have days when we feel bored, overloaded, or unappreciated, and dragging ourselves out of bed requires the strength of Hercules. However, if you feel like this most of the time, you're probably burned out!

> *If constant stress has you feeling disillusioned, helpless, and exhausted, you may be suffering from burnout.*

Here are some suggestions for conquering burnout. When I say suggestions, what I'm really saying is, do them now!

1. Take an extended break.

There is an old saying, "Everything in moderation." That includes work. Burnout is often a loud and clear signal that you need to take a break. Take a sabbatical, even if it is just for a few days. But here is the key: it must be a complete break. No laptop, no iPad, no cell phone, no nothing. You and your team must decide the appropriate length of time for your absence, depending on how deep your burnout is and how long the church can fill the gap. I've seen some pastors take as long as a two-year break. There is nothing wrong with that as long as it fits with the flow of your ministry at the time. For some, your sabbatical may be much shorter. Get away by yourself or with your family and recharge.

2. Stop devaluing yourself.

Burnout can occur when you're not feeling valued by others, but even more often when you devalue yourself. Take a few minutes to jot down the reasons you entered the ministry in the first place. Who are you really committed to serving? Write down how your current role makes a positive impact, whether on your congregation, your staff, or your family, as well as others in your life. Sometimes to press the reset button, you need to take a step back and remind yourself of your contributions — big or small — and recommit to the mission to which God has called you. Trying to please everybody and getting hung up on their approval can make you lose that perspective.

3. Adjust your vision.

In the end, burnout might be a sign that you need to make a change. This change could be either big or small. It could mean asking God for a new vision for your personal life or ministry, or both. It might mean that you need to add more fun time to your weekly calendar with people you love to be around. Or it might mean that you need to start thinking about a bigger vision for your ministry. Maybe you're feeling constrained. Whatever it is, don't be afraid to adjust your plans and see if you can find a different approach for this season of your life. In the end, God wants you to be happy at what you are doing, and maybe you just need to rethink your daily life now and add in some new wine into an old wineskin!

FOOD FOR YOUR SOUL

Matthew 11:28–30

"Come to me, all who are weary and heavy-laden, and I will give you rest. "Take my yoke upon you and learn from me, for I am gentle and humble in heart, and you will find rest for your souls. For my yoke is easy and my burden is light."

Galatians 6:9

"Let us not lose heart in doing good, for in due time we will reap if we do not grow weary."

Isaiah 40:28–31

"Do you not know? Have you not heard? The Lord is the everlasting God, the Creator of the ends of the earth. He will not grow tired or weary, and his understanding no one can fathom. He gives strength to the weary and increases the power of the weak. Even youths grow tired and weary, and young men stumble and fall; but those who hope in the Lord will renew their strength. They will soar on wings like eagles; they will run and not grow weary, they will walk and not be faint."

FOOD FOR THOUGHT

"Leadership is an active role; 'lead' is a verb. But the leader who tries to do it all is headed for burnout, and in a powerful hurry." — Bill Owens

"You're through. Finished. Burned out. Used up. You've been replaced. . . forgotten. That's a lie!" —Charles R. Swindoll

"God will never give you anything you can't handle, so don't stress." —Kelly Clarkson

DEVOTIONAL

The devotional portion of this chapter comes in the form of three basic questions:

1. What is really motivating me?

When busy and weary, we need to re-examine our motivation and why we are finding it so difficult to take a break. The most revealing question is not, "Why am I doing this?" but "Why can't I say 'no' to [or pause from] seemingly good or important things if they are having a negative impact on my physical and emotional wellbeing, my devotional and spiritual health, and relationships with those who matter to me?"

List three reasons you have trouble saying "no" to requests, even when they are having a negative impact on your life.

_____

_____

_____

_____

2. Am I being replenished?

Staying filled and energized does not come automatically. It takes time and intention. This does not only relate to times of trial. Even positive emotions, such as excitement about the ministry, can deplete you emotionally, and you need to pay attention to re-charging during those times, as well. Ask yourself, "Am I keeping the Sabbath principle?" God gave us the Sabbath rest for a purpose.

List the activities, people, and places that replenish you personally. Are you investing in them? Why or why not?

_____

_____

_____

_____

3. How are my personal "tank" levels? We all have an emotional tank that runs low when we get burned out. Sometimes we feel that we're running on empty. We need to be continually aware of this tank and keep it full so we have the reserves to meet each day's needs and demands. Self-awareness does not always come easily, but it is something we have to grow in if we are going to prevent burnout.

On a scale of 1 to 5, rank your tank levels in the following areas:

_____ Emotional health

_____ Mental / ability to think clearly and concentrate

_____ Physical health and energy

_____ Spiritual condition

_____ Energy to invest in your closest personal relationships

What steps can you take right now to refill your tank in each of these areas?

Emotional health :

_____

_____

_____

_____

Mental health:

_____

_____

_____

_____

Physical health:

_____

_____

_____

_____

Spiritual health:

_____

_____

_____

_____

Relational health:

_____

_____

_____

_____